D1267328

SIMPLE WEAVES
Over 30 Classic Patterns and Fresh New Styles

Birgitta Bengtsson Björk   Tina Ignell   *Photos:* Bengt Arne Ignell

SIMPLE WEAVES

Over 30 Classic Patterns and Fresh New Styles

TRAFALGAR SQUARE
North Pomfret, Vermont

Thank you

To the Handcraft Shop in Östergötland for allowing us
to use their location for the photos and to everyone who
opened their homes to us for photo shoots.

First published in the United States of America in 2012 by
Trafalgar Square Books
North Pomfret, Vermont 05053
www.trafalgarbooks.com

Originally published in Swedish as *Nya Vävar* by Forma Books AB

ISBN: 978-1-57076-555-1

Library of Congress Control Number: 2012934272

WEAVING DESIGNS AND TEXT: Birgitta Bengtsson Björk and Tina Ignell
PHOTOGRAPHY: Bengt Arne Ignell
ENGLISH TRANSLATION: Carol Huebscher Rhoades
TECHNICAL EDITOR: Becky Ashenden
SWEDISH EDITOR: Gunilla Wagner
DESIGN: Alexandra Frank
LAYOUT AND COPY: Britt-Marie Ström

Printed in China

10 9 8 7 6 5 4 3 2 1

Contents

Preface

It all began with a general warp in red and white for the runners, hand towels, placemats and pillows we asked designer Birgitta Bengtsson Björk to weave for VÄV–Scandinavian weaving magazine. When the weavings were finished, we saw that the pattern was also suitable for a blanket. Ideas began to take root and grow and we decided that we would work together to create a book where design is intertwined with information about weaving techniques and materials. It would be an inspiring textbook beginning with plain weave and twill and finishing with Block Damask (True Dräll) patterns.

When we each began our career paths many years ago, our first basic weaving classes were taught with a method similar to the approach in this book, so we thought it would be a good starting point. However, we wanted to do it our way.

Now that the book is ready to be used, we can look back at an intense period of discussions, test weaving, and countless decisions. Birgitta's designs has been, of course, the starting point. She focuses on simplicity, projects that are easy to learn, and designs that are timeless.

"Whatever you weave should be of high quality" is a comment we frequently make when working on our weavings. It should be fun to sit at the loom. Many of the weaves invite variations so that you can, as the weaver, easily create your own color choices.

CLASSIC PATTERNS FOR NEW WEAVES

The Monk's Belt pattern offers endless possibilities on the same warp for your own color choices; for example, the checked plain weave rug with closely set white stripes can be woven with blue, red or black checks. Perhaps you'll find inspiration for your own variations in a completely different weaving in the book.

Our goal is to show how the various techniques offer many options for a completely new weaving, sometimes in rather unexpected materials.

A spot weave, which is often used for fine curtains, can be woven in a black and white color pattern. You can play with the technique to weave fine wool pillows or widen the warp to weave a lovely blanket, perhaps in a totally different colorway.

Or, waffle weave, an obvious choice for a hand towel, can also be effective for a heavy rug, a soft wool pillow, or a cotton bath towel.

Damask, a pattern often woven in 100% linen or a linen blend, is transformed when woven with wool yarns for a billowy blanket, a checkerboard rug, or sheer curtains.

The possibilities are endless and once you are underway, we hope you'll find even more variations on your own.

Weaving means you can participate in an inspiring process from yarn to finished product. We hope that everyone who comes along for the journey will be happy to take part. We feel confident that the weavings presented in this book will provide many satisfying hours at the loom.

Birgitta studied at Konstfack (University College of Arts, Crafts, and Design) in Stockholm, Sweden and has many years of experience designing for the textile industry. Tina studied in the advanced handcraft program at Handarbetets Vänner (Friends of Handcraft), also in Stockholm. She has worked in handcrafts and, since 2004, been the editor of Vävmagasinet (the Scandinavian Weaving Magazine).

Birgitta Bengtsson Björk, Tina Ignell

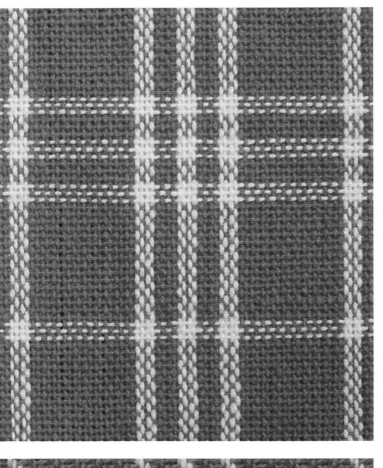

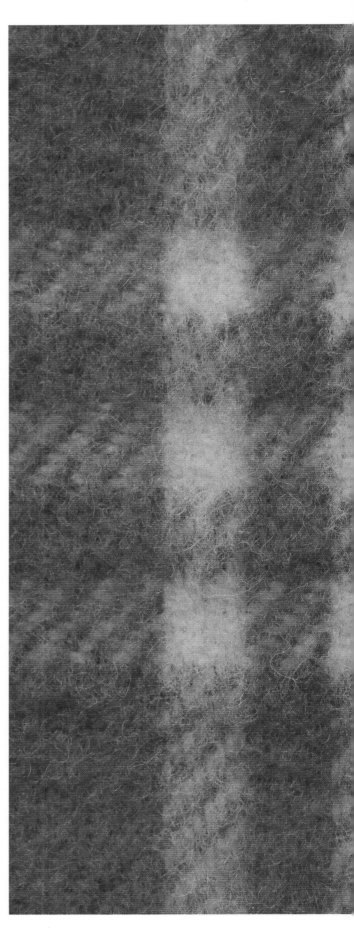

Plain Weave and Twill

Plain weave and twill can easily be woven on the same warp. Use a straight threading, from shafts 1 to 4 and change the tie-up. Plain weave is the tightest weave with the most "interlacement points possible" and, for that reason, is a little firmer than twill.

In the following weaving patterns, you'll find the basic design for hand towels and other projects has also inspired a blanket and a rug.

Checked and Striped hand towels woven with Nialin, pp. 14-19.

Checks and Stripes Woven in Nialin

For plain weave you only need two shafts, but, if you thread onto four shafts you can weave plain weave and various twills on the same warp. Weave striped and checked fabrics for pillows, runners, table mats, and hand towels.

TECHNIQUE
Plain weave, 4 shafts and 2 or 4 treadles

MATERIALS

WARP	22/2 Nialin
	red 2066, half-bleached 2000,
	6,600 m/kg Bockens Yarns,
	Holma-Helsingland
WEFT	Same yarn as for warp
REED	50/10 (12/in), 1 end per heddle, 2 ends per dent = 10 ends/1 cm (25 epi)
SELVEDGES	3 ends per dent 4 times on each side
WIDTH IN REED	51.5 cm (20 ¼ in)
FINISHED WIDTH	plain weave 49 cm (19 ¼ in) / twill approx. 48.5 cm (19 in)
WEFT PICKS	plain weave 7 picks/1 cm (17.5 ppi); twill 10 picks/1 cm (25 ppi)
NUMBER OF ENDS	524
WARP REQUIRED	Per meter: 63 g (2.2 oz) red, 20 g (.7 oz) half-bleached
WEFT REQUIRED	Per meter: single color plain weave 55 g (1.9 oz); single color twill approx. 80 g (2.8 oz)

WEAVING
Use a temple and move it up frequently. Choose the tie-up you want. Plain weave makes a more stable fabric and the weft doesn't beat in very tightly. Twill produces a softer weave and you can weave more picks per cm (inch).

Weave following the suggestions for the weft sequence (see pages 15-16) or design your own. Measure the first square and see how many picks are needed. After that count the picks for each square to establish a good rhythm so you only have to stop weaving to advance warp or change colors. It doesn't matter if the squares vary a bit in length. A little irregularity gives the finished hand towel or pillow a livelier surface.

When you are weaving tightly spaced, narrow stripes you can carry the second weft color along the selvedge.

FINISHING
After you've finished weaving the yardage, all you have to do is sew the pieces into pillows, covers, table mats, runners or hand towels.
1. Plain weave runner with the same squares as in the warp, 49 x 200 cm (19 ¼ x 78 ¾ in).
2. Plain weave hand towel with wide squares, 49 x 70 cm (19 ¼ x 27 ½ in).
3. Striped hand towel in plain weave with red weft, 49 x 70 cm (19 ¼ x 27 ½ in).
4. Twill pillow with the same squares as the warp, 46 x 46 cm (18 ¼ x 18 ¼ in).
5. Two twill table mats with widely spaced squares, 48 x 38 cm (19 x 15 in).
6. Twill hand towel with closely spaced squares, 48 x 70 cm (19 x 27 ½ in).
7. Striped pillow in point twill, red weft. (The pillows are fastened with 5 white snaps on the back.)

LIKE-SIDED TWILL 4 3 2 1

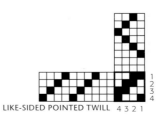

LIKE-SIDED POINTED TWILL 4 3 2 1

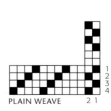

PLAIN WEAVE 2 1

WARP SEQUENCE

RED	28		4		4		20		20		4		4		28	= 400
WHITE		4		4		4		4		4		4		4		= 124

× 7

= 524 ENDS

WEFT SEQUENCE 1
PLAIN WEAVE, THE SAME SQUARES AS IN THE WARP

RED		3		3		16		16
WHITE	3		3		3		3	

REPEAT

WEFT SEQUENCE 2
PLAIN WEAVE, WIDE SQUARES

RED	22		22		
WHITE		3		3	

REPEAT

WEFT SEQUENCE 3
PLAIN WEAVE, WEFT IS ALL RED

WEFT SEQUENCE 4
TWILL, THE SAME SQUARES AS IN THE WARP

RED		4		4		20		20
WHITE	4		4		4		4	

REPEAT

WEFT SEQUENCE 5
TWILL WITH WIDE SQUARES

RED	32		32		
WHITE		4		4	

REPEAT

WEFT SEQUENCE 6
TWILL WITH CLOSELY SET SQUARES

RED	20		20		
WHITE		20		20	

REPEAT

WEFT SEQUENCE 7
POINT TWILL, WEFT IS ALL RED

HAND TOWEL HANGING LOOP

WARP	22/2 Nialin, the same yarn as for the hand towels
WEFT	22/2 Nialin, red
FINISHED WIDTH	1 cm (3/8 in)
WOVEN LENGTH	10 cm (4 in) / hanging loop
WEFT PICKS	approx. 10 picks/2 cm (12.5 ppi)
NUMBER OF ENDS	24

WARP SEQUENCE

RED	2		4		4		2	=12 ENDS
WHITE		4		4		4		=12 ENDS

Red and White Checked Twill Blanket

This wool blanket, woven in a warm red and white, was inspired by the checked hand towels.

TECHNIQUE
Like-sided twill, 4 shafts and 4 treadles

MATERIALS

WARP	Tuna 6/2 wool white 3001, red 3318 approx. 3,100 m/kg Borg's Weaving Yarns
WEFT	Same yarn as for warp
REED	30/10 (8/in), 1 end per heddle, 2 ends per dent = 6 ends/1 cm (15 epi)
SELVEDGES	3 ends per dent 2 times at each side
WIDTH IN REED	145 cm (57 in)
WOVEN LENGTH	approx. 200 cm (78 ¾ in)
FINISHED MEASUREMENTS	approx. 135 x 205 cm (53 ¼ x 80 ¾ in)
WEFT SETT	6 picks/1 cm (15 ppi) measured under tension
NUMBER OF ENDS	876
WARP REQUIRED	Per meter: white 70 g (2.5 oz), red 215 g (7.5 oz)

WEFT REQUIRED For each blanket: white 110 g (3.85 oz), red 390 g (13.7 oz)

WEAVING
Use a temple and move it up frequently. Begin by weaving a 10 cm (4 in) header. Advance the warp, leaving about 30 cm (11 ¾ in) unwoven. Weave a short length of the first blanket. Twist each fringe with 8 ends, 4 ends in each hand. If you are weaving several blankets, leave 30 cm (11 ¾ in) for the fringe on each blanket. Twist the fringes on the loom.

FINISHING
Make sure that any knots are untied and woven correctly into the fabric before sending the blanket(s) out for finishing.

WARP SEQUENCE

RED	34		8		8		40		40		8		8		34	660
WHITE		8		8		8		8		8		8		8		216

128 × 6
= 768 ENDS

= 876 ENDS

WEFT SEQUENCE IN MILLIMETERS

RED	65		12		12		65		65		12		12		65
WHITE		12		12		12		12		12		12		12	

20.2 CM X 9 = 182 CM
(8 IN X 9 = 72 IN)

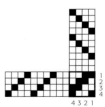

Checked Rug in Loose and Tight Plain Weave

The pattern changes a bit more...into a rug where the white stripes are sleyed closely together; with the white weft you can easily weave a checked rug.

TECHNIQUE
Plain weave, 4 shafts and 2 treadles

MATERIALS

WARP	12/6 Cotton warp bleached + black 522, 2,950 m/kg Bockens Yarns, Holma-Helsingland
WEFT	Hems: 1 cm (3/8 in) wide blue rags Rug: white and blue rags, approx. 2 cm (¾ in) wide
REED	30/10 (8/in) black warp threaded 1 end per heddle, 1 end per dent white warp threaded 1 end per heddle, 2 ends per dent
SELVEDGES	2 ends per dent 2 times at each side
WIDTH IN REED	61 cm (24 in)
FINISHED WIDTH	approx. 59 cm (23 ¼ in)
WEFT SETT	3 picks/1 cm (7.5 ppi) measured under tension
NUMBER OF ENDS	220 (148 black, 72 white)
WARP REQUIRED	Per meter: 50 g (1.8 oz) black, 25 g (.88 oz) white
WEFT REQUIRED	Per meter: approx. 600 g (21.1 oz) blue + white rags for stripes

WEAVING
Use a temple and move it up frequently. Arc the rags well and make sure that the weft is packed evenly between the tight white stripes. Weave approx. 6 cm (2 ½ in) for the hem with the 1 cm (3/8 in) wide rags and then weave following the weft sequence to desired length.

FINISHING
Knot every 4 warp ends together in an overhand knot. Fold down as close to the knots as possible and sew down hems by hand.

WEFT SEQUENCE
6 cm (2 ½ in) hem with 1 cm (3/8 in) wide blue rags
6 cm (2 ½ in) with blue rags
3 picks white ⎫
9 cm (3 ½ in) with blue rags ⎬ repeat
3 picks white ⎭
6 cm (2 ½ in) with blue rags
6 cm (2 ½ in) hem with 1 cm (⅜ in) wide blue rags

THREADING IN HEDDLES:
BLACK: 1 END PER HEDDLE
WHITE: 1 END PER HEDDLE

REED:
BLACK: 1 END PER DENT
WHITE: 2 ENDS PER DENT

1
2
3
4

2 1

WARP SEQUENCE

BLACK	22	20	6	6	20	20	6	6	20	22		= 148
WHITE		8	8	8	8	8	8	8	8	8		= 72

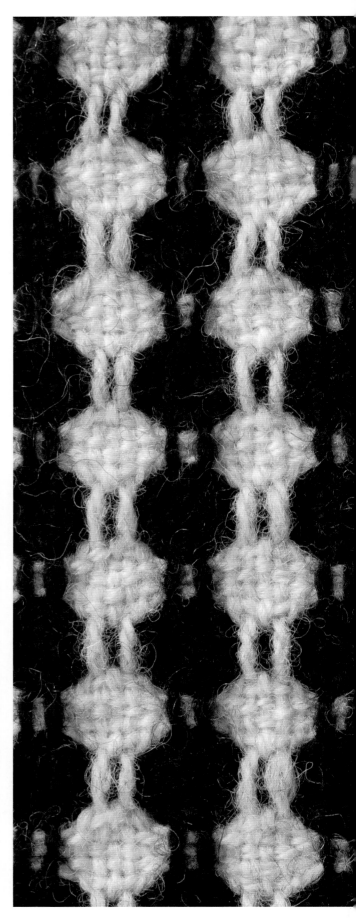

Canvas and
Spot Weaves

*Canvas weaves feature small open spaces and are often
used for curtains. By using other materials and weaving
more tightly the floats create exciting plaited effects.*

*In this chapter, a linen placemat and a pillow are woven
with two qualities of tow linen, both in canvas weave, but
completely different from each other.*

*When woven with wool yarn, the spot weave floats create
a surprising motif in black and white.*

Canvas Weave Placemats

When placemats are woven with lovely, thick linen tow yarns, the canvas weave forms a fine braid pattern.

TECHNIQUE
Canvas weave, 4 shafts and 4 treadles

MATERIALS

WARP	Half-bleached 1.5 linen tow, or black 1.5 linen tow approx. 900 m/kg Bocken's Yarns, Holma-Helsingland
WEFT	Same yarn as for warp
REED	45/10 (12/in), 1 end per heddle, 1 end per dent = 4.5 ends/1 cm (11.25 epi)
WIDTH IN REED	38 cm (15 in)
FINISHED WIDTH	approx. 38 cm (15 in)
WEFT SETT	approx. 5-6 picks/1 cm (12.5-15 ppi)
NUMBER OF ENDS	170
WARP REQUIRED	Per meter: approx. 200 g (7 oz)
WEFT REQUIRED	Per meter: approx. 250 g (8.8 oz)

WEAVING
Use treadles 2 and 3 to weave a 2 cm (3/4 in) hem. Weave approx. 46 cm (18 ¼ in) following the treadling order. Finish with a hem.

Wind the yarn on a stick shuttle and throw 1 pick at a time even on the sections with four picks in the same shed. Bring the weft around the outermost warp end and carefully enter it back into the same shed. Use a controlled beat to pack the weft into the weaving, making sure weft density is correct.

Sew down the hems by hand with closely spaced stitches or machine-stitch. Soak mats in water and then lay flat to dry.

Cleaning: Hand wash and dry flat.

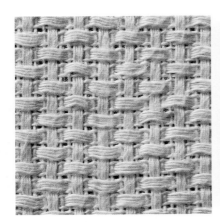

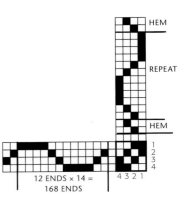

HEM

REPEAT

HEM

1
2
3
4

12 ENDS × 14 = 168 ENDS

4 3 2 1

Canvas weave placemat,
page 27.

Canvas Weave Linen Pillows

Canvas weave with a finer yarn makes a totally different fabric. With white at the sides and yellow in the center you can produce an elegant frame. The whole pillow was woven with doubled weft.

TECHNIQUE
Canvas weave, 4 shafts and 4 treadles

MATERIALS

WARP	6/1 linen tow
	half-bleached, yellow 105, 4,200 m/kg
	Bocken's Yarns, Holma-Helsingland
WEFT	Doubled 6/1 linen tow
REED	40/10 (10/in), 1 end per heddle, 2 ends
	per dent = 8 ends/1 cm (20 epi)
WIDTH IN REED	43.5 cm (17 in)
FINISHED WIDTH	approx. 42 cm (16 ½ in)
WEFT SETT	1 repeat/6 doubled weft picks = 1 cm
	(⅜ in);
NUMBER OF ENDS	348 (172 white, 176 yellow)
WARP REQUIRED	Per meter: approx. 45 g (1.6 oz) white,
	45 g (1.6 oz) yellow
WEFT REQUIRED	Per pillow cover: approx. 55 g (1.9 oz)
	white, 55 g (1.9 oz) yellow

WEAVING
Weave following the weft sequence.

FINISHING
Fold fabric for each pillow at the center, sew the side seams and insert a pillow form (40 x 40 cm/15 ¾ x 15 ¾ in). Fold under a 3 cm (1 ¼ in) selvedge and seam open sides.

WEFT SEQUENCE FOR ONE PILLOW COVER
3 cm (1 ¼ in) plain weave on treadles 2 and 3
10 cm (4 in) white following treadling sequence
22 cm (8 ¾ in) yellow following treadling sequence
20 cm (8 in) white following treadling sequence
22 cm (8 ¾ in) yellow following treadling sequence
10 cm (4 in) white following treadling sequence
3 cm (1 ¼ in) plain weave on treadles 2 and 3

WARP SEQUENCE

WHITE	86		86	= 172
YELLOW		176		= 176

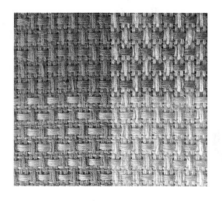

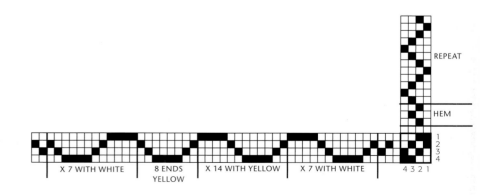

Black and White Wool Fabric in Spot Weave

In spot weave, the warp and weft threads float around a plain weave background. In this black and white pillow the black and white ends follow the weave structure and reinforce the pattern.

TECHNIQUE
Spot weave, 4 shafts and 4 treadles

MATERIALS

WARP	Tuna 6/2 wool
	white 3001, black 3099
	approx. 3,100 m/kg
	Borg's Weaving Yarns
WEFT	same as for warp
REED	25/10 (6/in), 1 end per heddle, 2 ends per dent = 5 ends/1 cm (12.5 epi)
WIDTH IN REED	53 cm (21 in)
FINISHED WIDTH	approx. 45 cm (17 ¾ in) after washing
WEFT SETT	approx. 6 picks/1 cm (15 ppi)
NUMBER OF ENDS	265 (135 black, 130 white)
WARP REQUIRED	Per meter: approx. 45 g (1.6 oz) black, 40 g (1.4 oz) white
WEFT REQUIRED	Per meter: approx. 55 g (1.9 oz) black, 50 g (1.8 oz) white

WEAVING
Warp with 1 end, 5 of each color. Weave following weft sequence.

FINISHING
Machine-wash on wool setting at 40°C (104°F). Fold fabric for each pillow at the center, sew the side seams and insert a pillow form (50 x 50 cm/19 ¾ x 19 ¾ in). Fold down selvedge and seam open sides.

WARP SEQUENCE

BLACK	5		5	= 135
WHITE		5		= 130
		× 26		

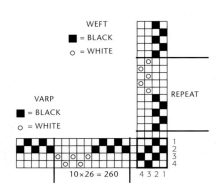

Monk's Belt and Honeycomb

Monk's belt is a pattern weave with floats on a plain weave background. If you use wool yarns the pattern makes a fine woven lining for a sheepskin rug or for some pretty pillows; with a non-wool yarn and a striped warp the colors have free play in the weaving. Become inspired and mix your own colors to vary the pattern. You can also weave honeycomb on the same threading as for monk's belt. We wove the honeycombs with a thick wool yarn for pretty pillows.

Woolen Weaves in Monk's Belt

Monk's belt woven entirely with wool yarns makes a lovely top for a sheepskin or some pretty floor cushions.

TECHNIQUE
Monk's Belt, 4 shafts and 4 treadles

MATERIALS

WARP	Tuna 6/2 wool yarn natural white 3001, approx. 3,100 m/kg Borg's Weaving Yarns
WEFT	Background: natural white as for warp, woven with single strand Pattern: woven with doubled yarn (weaving on the sheepskin) medium gray 3023, black 3099, dark blue 3328, wine red 3321
REED	30/10 (8/in), 1 end per heddle, 2 ends per dent = 6 ends/1 cm (15 epi)
WIDTH IN REED	60 cm (23 ¾ in)
FINISHED WIDTH	approx. 57 cm (22 ½ in)
WEFT SETT	4 plain weave picks + 4 pattern picks/1 cm (3/8 in)
NUMBER OF ENDS	358
WARP REQUIRED	Per meter: approx. 120 g (4.2 oz)
WEFT REQUIRED	Per meter: Plain weave: 80 g (2.8 oz) natural white, approx. 25 g (.88 oz) black, dark blue, and wine red

WEAVING

Thread following the pattern draft. Divide the yarns into warp groups following the thread count for each group before you begin threading. Weave following the weft sequence.

SEWING TO THE SHEEPSKIN

Lay the woven fabric over the sheepskin and pin securely. Cut the skin exactly the same size as the weaving. Hold the wool so that the locks won't be cut off accidentally. Lay the fabric on the wool side of the skin. Tie linen threads at several places at the sides before you begin sewing so that the skin doesn't pull in while you are stitching. Sew firmly with small running stitches (up and down) through the fabric and skin. Leave approx. 20 cm (8 in) open. Turn inside out so that the wool side is on the outside. If you want a pelt pillow insert a pillow form before you close the opening.
Note Be careful to hold the wool to the right side so that the edge will be as wooly as possible.

WEFT SEQUENCE FOR WOOL FABRIC ON A SHEEPSKIN

Weave plain weave with white yarn for approx. 4 cm (1 ½ in)

5 pattern wefts black on treadle 1
5 pattern wefts gray on treadle 4
1 pattern weft gray on treadle 1
5 pattern wefts gray on treadle 4
5 pattern wefts blue on treadle 1
5 pattern wefts gray on treadle 4
1 pattern weft gray on treadle 1
5 pattern wefts gray on treadle 4
5 pattern wefts wine red on treadle 1
5 pattern wefts gray on treadle 4
1 pattern weft gray on treadle 1
5 pattern wefts gray on treadle 4

} Repeat to desired length

Between each pattern weft, weave a plain weave shot with white.

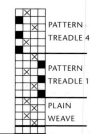

8 ENDS   18 ENDS   36 × 9 = 324 ENDS   8 ENDS   4 3 2 1

Monk's Belt Variations

Stripes in the warp provide a good rhythm for the pattern. By using the same treadling with various color combinations you can create a number of weaves on the same warp. See also the runner and pillows on pages 40-41.

TECHNIQUE
Monk's belt, 4 shafts and 4 treadles

MATERIALS

WARP	22/2 Nialin half-bleached 2000 + black 2005, 6,600 m/kg Bocken's Yarns, Holma-Helsingland
WEFT	Background: half-bleached as for warp, woven with a single strand Pattern: Woven with doubled yarn Yarn for variations: See under the corresponding weft sequence Black 2005, gray 2003, brown 2049, lime 2041, orange 2014, red 2080
REED	50/10 (12/in), 1 end per heddle, 2 ends per dent = 10 ends/1 cm (25 epi)
WIDTH IN REED	54.6 cm (21 ½ in)
FINISHED WIDTH	approx. 52 cm (20 ½ in)
WEFT SETT	5 plain weave picks + 5 pattern picks/1 cm (3/8 in)
NUMBER OF ENDS	546
WARP REQUIRED	Per meter: approx. 52 g (1.8 oz) half-bleached, 32 g (1.1 oz) black

WEFT REQUIRED   Per meter: background 42 g (1.5 oz) half-bleached
Pattern:
Runner, p. 39: approx. 35 g (1.2 oz) gold brown, 35 g (1.2 oz) gray, 20 g (.7 oz) black
Runner, p. 40: 70 g (2.5 oz) black, 30 g (1 oz) red
Pillows, p. 41:
1. 100 g (3.5 oz) black
2. 70 g (2.5 oz) black, 30 g (1 oz) lime
3. 70 g (2.5 oz) brown, 30 g (1 oz) black
4. 70 g (2.5 oz) lime, 30 g (1 oz) orange

WEAVING AND FINISHING
Thread following the pattern draft. Divide the warp yarns up following the thread counts for each group before you begin threading. Weave following the weft sequence.

WARP SEQUENCE

BLACK	4	18		22		= 206
HALF-BLEACHED			34			= 340

× 10

WARP
■ = BLACK
○ = HALF-BLEACHED

WEFT SEQUENCE FOR RUNNER SHOWN ON PAGE 39

Black:	5 pattern picks treadle 1	⎫
Brown:	5 pattern picks treadle 4	
	5 pattern picks treadle 1	
	1 pattern pick treadle 4	⎬ 1 repeat
	5 pattern picks treadle 1	
	5 pattern picks treadle 4	⎭
Black:	5 pattern picks treadle 1	
Gray:	5 pattern picks treadle 4	
	5 pattern picks treadle 1	
	1 pattern pick treadle 4	
	5 pattern picks treadle 1	
	5 pattern picks treadle 4	

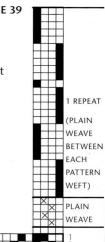

1 REPEAT
(PLAIN WEAVE BETWEEN EACH PATTERN WEFT)

PLAIN WEAVE

1
2
3
4

52 × 10 = 520 ENDS

4 3 2 1

WEFT SEQUENCE FOR BLACK AND RED RUNNER

Red:	5 pattern picks treadle 1
Black:	5 pattern picks treadle 4
	5 pattern picks treadle 1
	1 pattern pick treadle 4
	5 pattern picks treadle 1
	5 pattern picks treadle 4

WEFT SEQUENCE FOR PILLOWS WORKED FROM THE TOP DOWN

1. BLACK:	The same weft sequence as 2-4 but using only black
2. LIME:	5 pattern picks treadle 1
	1 pattern pick treadle 4
	5 pattern picks treadle 1
Black:	5 pattern picks treadle 4
3. BROWN:	5 pattern picks treadle 1
	1 pattern pick treadle 4
	5 pattern picks treadle 1
Black:	5 pattern picks treadle 4
4. LIME:	5 pattern picks treadle 1
	1 pattern pick treadle 4
	5 pattern picks treadle 1
Orange:	5 pattern picks treadle 4

Honeycomb in Striped Woolen Weave

Honeycomb can be woven on the same threading as for monk's belt. The finer weft yarn fills different blocks with a tight plain weave, while those that don't interlace in the plain weave float on the back of the fabric. A thick weft is thrown in between the honeycomb cells to form a wavy pattern.

TECHNIQUE
Honeycomb, 4 shafts and 6 treadles

MATERIALS

WARP	Tuna 6/2 wool yarn, approx. 3,100 m/kg turquoise 3718, natural white 3001 Borg's Weaving Yarns
WEFT	Plain weave: woven on the back and in the honeycombs single strand indigo blue 3748, light blue 3329 thick plain weave weft between the honeycombs: doubled yarn, natural white 3001
REED	25/10 (6/in), 1 end per heddle, 2 ends per dent = 5 ends/1 cm (12.5 epi)
WIDTH IN REED	54 cm (21 ¼ in)
FINISHED WIDTH	51 cm (20 in) honeycomb weaving 52 cm (20 ½ in) plain weave
WEFT SETT	plain weave 6 picks/1 cm (15 ppi)
NUMBER OF ENDS	270 (144 turquoise, 126 white)
WARP REQUIRED	Per meter: approx. 50 g (1.8 oz) turquoise, 41 g (1.4 oz) white
WEFT REQUIRED	Per meter: plain weave 105 g (3.7 oz) (approx. 50 g (1.8 oz)/color) honeycomb approx. 50 g (1.8 oz) natural white

WEAVING
Weave following the weft sequence. The front is woven in honeycomb and the back in plain weave.

FINISHING
Fold fabric for each pillow at the center and sew the side seams. Insert a 50 x 50 cm (19 ¾ x 19 ¾ in) pillow form. Fold under a 1 ¼" selvedge and seam the open side.

WEFT SEQUENCE FOR A PILLOW COVER
5 cm (2 in) plain weave with single strand light blue, treadles 1+2
6 picks single light blue, treadles 5+6

2 picks doubled natural white, treadles 1+2 ⎫
12 picks single strand indigo blue, treadles 3+4 ⎬ repeat
2 picks doubled natural white, treadles 1+2
12 picks single strand light blue, treadles 5+6 ⎭

2 picks doubled natural white, treadles 1+2
12 picks single strand indigo blue, treadles 3+4
2 picks doubled natural white, treadles 1+2
6 picks single strand light blue, treadles 5+6

Weave the back of the pillow cover in plain weave with a single strand of light blue yarn on treadles 1 and 2.

WARP SEQUENCE

TURQUOISE	18		18	= 144
NATURAL WHITE		18		= 126
		× 7		

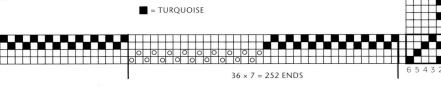

WARP
○ = NATURAL WHITE
■ = TURQUOISE

HONEY-COMB II
HONEY-COMB I
PLAIN WEAVE

36 × 7 = 252 ENDS

6 5 4 3 2 1

Rosepath

Rosepath makes just what it promises – ethereal flower shapes and it's fun to weave and vary. A narrow border with small roses yields three weaves: a pillow with soft roses, either striped or an overall pattern, a hand towel with fine red rose borders, and a pretty linen rug with rose stripes.

Pillow Woven in Rosepath

In a plain weave with three strands held together for the warp and weft, the rosepath pattern is formed with the softest velour yarn. Weave rosepath borders or an overall pattern.

TECHNIQUE
Rosepath, 4 shafts and 6 treadles

MATERIALS

WARP	22/2 Cottolin black 209, approx. 6,400 m/kg Borg's Weaving Yarns
WEFT	Background: cottolin as for warp, 3 strands held together Pattern: single strand velour yarn, natural 1000, approx. 1,800 m/kg Borg's Weaving Yarns
REED	35/10 (9/in), 3 ends per heddle, 3 ends per dent = 10.5 ends/1 cm (26.25 epi)
WIDTH IN REED	56 cm (22 in)
FINISHED WIDTH	approx. 52 cm (20 ½ in)
WEFT SETT	Plain weave, 4 tripled picks/1 cm (10 tripled ppi) Rosepath, 4 plain weave picks + 4 pattern picks/1 cm (3/8 in)
NUMBER OF ENDS	591
WARP REQUIRED	Per meter: approx. 95 g (3.3 oz) black
WEFT REQUIRED	Per meter: plain weave approx. 110 g (3.85 oz) black cottolin approx. 125 g (4.4 oz) velour yarn for an allover pattern

WEAVING
Each pillow has a finished measurement of 50 x 50 cm (19 ¾ x 19 ¾ in). The front and back are woven at the same time = approx. 110 cm (43 ¼ in).

Weave following the weft sequence.

FINISHING
Fold in the hems and machine stitch. Fold the pillow, overlapping the hems so that the top is uppermost. Sew on 5-6 snaps. Turn the pillow wrong side out.

Machine-stitch each side seam.

Make sure that the pillow cover is 50 cm (19 ¾ in) wide. Button up and turn the cover right side out. Insert pillow form. The side with the snaps is the right side.

WEFT SEQUENCE FOR ONE PILLOW COVER
5 cm (2 in) hem in plain weave with 3 strands black cottolin
60 cm (23 ¾ in) with tightly woven rosepath, see treadling sequence
= 11 cm (4 ¼ in) pocket and 49 cm (19 ¼ in) back.
3 cm plain weave with 3 strands black cottolin
Rosepath following treadling sequence ⎫
4.5 cm (1 ¾ in) plain weave ⎬ x 6 = 36 cm
6 cm (2 ½ in) hem in plain weave ⎭ (14 ¼ in)

THE SECOND PILLOW IS WOVEN MIRROR IMAGE
5 cm (2 in) hem in plain weave with 3 strands black cottolin
4.5 cm (1 ¾ in) plain weave ⎫ x 10 = 60 cm
Rosepath following ⎬ (23 ¾ in)
treadling sequence ⎭
3 cm (1 ¼ in) plain weave
tightly woven rosepath for approx. 39 cm (15 ½ in)
finish with 3 cm (1 ¼ in) hem in plain weave

WEFT
o = 1 STRAND VELOUR YARN
■ = 3 STRANDS COTTOLIN

TIGHTLY WOVEN ROSEPATH, WORK REPEAT

ROSEPATH BORDER

PLAIN WEAVE

WARP
■ = 3 STRANDS COTTOLIN

9 ENDS   21 ENDS   24 x 23 = 552 ENDS   9 ENDS   6 5 4 3 2 1

1 2 3 4

Pillows woven in rosepath, p. 47.

Linen rug with rosepath borders, p. 53.

Striped Hand Towels with Rosepath Patterns

The rosepath makes fine narrow borders for these hand towels, woven entirely with cotton. The plain weave picks between the rosepath patterns are omitted in the borders and thus the pattern could also be called *korndräll* (a type of diamond twill) – that's how it goes in the weaving world.

TECHNIQUE
Rosepath/korndräll, 4 shafts and 6 treadles

MATERIALS

WARP	16/2 cotton bleached, 12,800 m/kg Borg's Weaving Yarns
WEFT	Background: plain weave with same yarn as warp Pattern: doubled 16/2 cotton red 290, Borg's Weaving Yarns
REED	70/10 (18/in), 1 end per heddle, 2 ends per dent = 14 ends/1 cm (35 epi)
WIDTH IN REED	approx. 49.5 cm (19 ½ in)
FINISHED WIDTH	approx. 48 cm (19 in)
WEFT SETT	Plain weave: 14 picks/1 cm (35 ppi) approx. 10 pattern picks with doubled yarn/1 cm (25 ppi)
NUMBER OF ENDS	695

WARP REQUIRED	Per meter: approx. 55 g (1.9 oz)
WEFT REQUIRED	Per meter: plain weave approx. 55 g (1.9 oz) + approx. 25 g (.88 oz) red for pattern

WEAVING
Weave a 5 cm (2 in) border following the treadling sequence. Weave 4 cm (1 ½ in) plain weave with white + a narrow rosepath stripe following the treadling sequence. Repeat until the towel is approx. 60 cm (23 ¾ in) long. Finish with 4 cm (1 ½ in) plain weave and a 5 cm (2 in) border.

FINISHING
Fold the edges under so that about 2 cm (3/4 in) of the border is used for a hem on each side. Sew down hems by hand. Weave a hanging loop in a similar pattern.

HANGING LOOP
6 ends bleached
6 ends red
6 ends bleached
Thread 1 bleached end per hole or slot
Thread 2 red ends per hole or slot

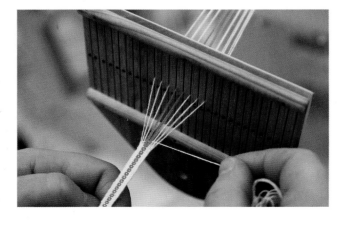

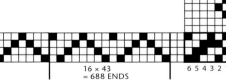

WEFT
o = DOUBLED 16/2 RED;
    NO PLAIN WEAVE PICKS
■ = PLAIN WEAVE, BLEACHED
    16/2 COTTON

NARROW ROSEPATH STRIPE

WIDE ROSEPATH BORDER

PLAIN WEAVE

16 × 43 = 688 ENDS

6 5 4 3 2 1

1
2
3
4

Linen Rug with Rosepath Stripes

The same rosepath stripe woven for the hand towels shown on page 50 is used here for a linen rug. You can weave a tighter background if, instead of plain weave, you weave with the pattern weft and alternate between the treadles that are woven opposite each other.

TECHNIQUE
Rosepath, 4 shafts and 4 treadles

MATERIALS

WARP	12/6 cotton rug warp
	black 522, 2,950 m/kg
	Bocken's Yarns, Holma-Helsingland
WEFT	Background: doubled unbleached
	4/6 rug linen, 400 m/kg
	Rosepath stripes: doubled half-bleached 4/6 rug linen, 400 m/kg
	8/5 linen warp for twisting the fringes
REED	30/10 (8/in), 1 end per heddle, 1 end per dent = 3 ends/1 cm (7.5 epi)
SELVEDGES	2 ends per dent on each side
WIDTH IN REED	approx. 61 cm (24 in)
FINISHED WIDTH	approx. 58 cm (22 ¾ in)
WEFT SETT	approx. 30 doubled picks/1 dm (7.5 epi)
NUMBER OF ENDS	183
WARP REQUIRED	Per meter: approx. 65 g (2.3 oz)
WEFT REQUIRED	Per meter: background approx. 900 g (2 lb); borders: approx. 200 g (7 oz)

WEAVING
Weave a short length with rags so that you can attach the temple. This section + the front ties will be used for the fringe. Follow the weft sequence.
Note Begin and end with treadle 4 before and after the pattern stripe for the best interlacement.

FINISHING
To make a more stable fringe, tie in 2 ends 8/5 linen warp yarn. Cut off two lengths, slightly over twice the length as the fringe. These are tied together with 8 rug warp ends with a single knot. Put half of the ends in each hand. Twist the fringe by turning the strands to the right and laying them to the left. Finish with two half hitches around the fringe.

WEFT SEQUENCE FOR ONE RUG
10 picks cotton rug warp, arc well
7 cm (2 ¾ in) background with unbleached rug linen
1 rosepath stripe with half-bleached rug linen ⎫
10 cm (4 in) background with unbleached rug linen ⎬ repeat
1 rosepath stripe with half-bleached rug linen ⎭
7 cm (2 ¾ in) background with unbleached rug linen
10 picks cotton rug warp

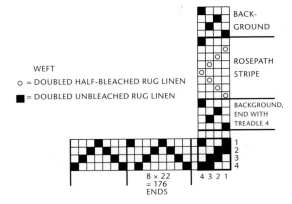

WEFT
o = DOUBLED HALF-BLEACHED RUG LINEN
■ = DOUBLED UNBLEACHED RUG LINEN

BACK-GROUND

ROSEPATH STRIPE

BACKGROUND, END WITH TREADLE 4

8 × 22 = 176 ENDS

4 3 2 1

1 2 3 4

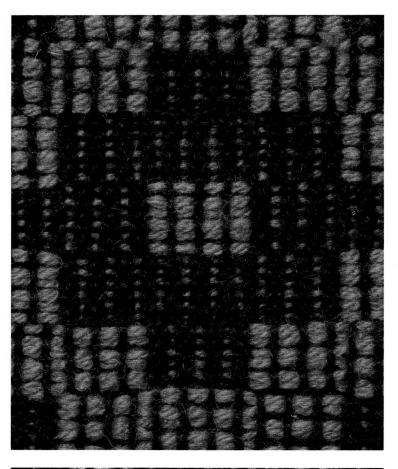

Overshot and Jämtlandsdräll (crackle)

Both of these patterns are simple block weaves with pattern floats on a plain weave background.

We wove the warm red overshot with light borders first and then picked a detail out of that weave to use for the next project, a blanket in Jämtlandsdräll. We chose yet another motif from the blanket and an asymmetrical linen rug grew out of it.

Overshot Runner

Overshot is woven with several pattern blocks. The runner shown here has three pattern treadles. What is particular to overshot is that the pattern weft goes in as plain weave between the floats, producing the characteristic halftones in the pattern.

TECHNIQUE
Overshot, 4 shafts and 5 treadles

MATERIALS

WARP	16/2 cotton, approx. 12,960 m/kg bleached and deep rose 518
	Bocken's Yarns, Holma-Helsingland
WEFT	Background: 16/2 cotton, deep rose 518. Pattern: doubled 16/2 cotton, red 1007 Bocken's Yarns, Holma-Helsingland
REED	80/10 (20/in), 1 end per heddle, 2 ends per dent = 16 ends/1 cm (40 epi)
SELVEDGES	3 ends per dent 2 times at each side
WIDTH IN REED	54 cm (21 ¼ in)
FINISHED WIDTH	approx. 51.5 cm (20 ¼ in)
WEFT SETT	approx. 10 plain weave and 10 pattern picks/1 cm (25+25 ppi)

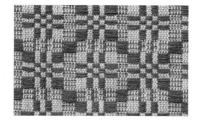

NUMBER OF ENDS 868

WARP REQUIRED Per meter: white approx. 25 g (.88 oz), rose approx. 45 g (1.6 oz)

WEFT REQUIRED Per meter: background approx. 40 g (1.4 oz) pattern approx. 80 g (2.8 oz)

WEAVING

Weave 2 cm (¾ in) in plain weave for the hem. Weave pattern following the treadling sequence until piece is desired length. Divide the warp into bundles following the pattern blocks before you begin to thread.

WARP SEQUENCE

WHITE	140		140	= 280
PINK		588		= 588

PATTERN BALANCING

RIGHT SELVEDGE	8 ENDS
GROUP I = 72 ENDS X 11	792 ENDS
GROUP II 60 ENDS	60 ENDS
LEFT SELVEDGE	8 ENDS
TOTAL	868 ENDS

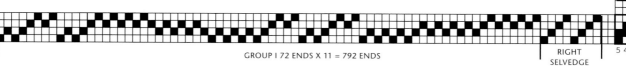

GROUP I 72 ENDS X 11 = 792 ENDS

RIGHT SELVEDGE

REPEAT TO DESIRED LENGTH

HEM

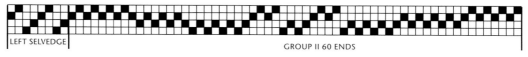

LEFT SELVEDGE

GROUP II 60 ENDS

Jämtlandsdräll (Crackle) Blanket

Like overshot, Jämtlandsdräll is a simple block weave with pattern floats on a plain weave background. Tie-down ends are used in the warp in order to reduce the size of the floats, which creates a sturdy fabric. You can weave some pillows on the same warp as the blanket, with one side woven with gray and the other with red.

TECHNIQUE
Jämtlandsdräll, 4 shafts and 6 treadles

MATERIALS

WARP	Tuna 6/2 wool yarn black 3099, approx. 3,100 m/kg Borg's Weaving Yarns
WEFT	Tuna 6/2 wool yarn Background: black 3099 Pattern: natural white 3001, doubled Borders: gray 3031, doubled
REED	30/10 (8/in), 1 end per heddle, 2 ends per dent = 6 ends/1 cm (15 epi)
WIDTH IN REED	Blanket: 130 cm (51 ¼ in) Pillow: 52 cm (20 ½ in) (width of pillow)
FINISHED WIDTH	Blanket: approx. 115 cm (45 ¼ in) after washing at 40°C/104°F Pillow: approx. 48 cm (19 in) after washing at 40°C/104°F
WEFT SETT	4-5 background + pattern picks/ 2 cm (¾ in)

NUMBER OF ENDS	Blanket: 780 Pillow: 312
WARP REQUIRED	Per meter: blanket 250 g (8.8 oz) Per meter: pillow approx. 110 g (3.85 oz)
WEFT REQUIRED	Per blanket: 180 g (6.3 oz) black, 110 g (3.85 oz) gray, 250 g (8.8 oz) white Per pillow: 150 g (5.3 oz) black, 150 g (5.3 oz) gray, 150 g (5.3 oz) red

WEAVING AND FINISHING

Blanket: Weave following the weft sequence. Zigzag the edges. Wash on wool cycle at 40°C/104°F. Edge each side with buttonhole stitch.

Pillows: Weave approx. 70 cm (27 ½ in) with each color following the treadling sequence for the pillows. Fold pillow fabric at the center. Sew the seams at the sides and insert a pillow form, 50 x 60 cm (19 ¾ x 23 ¾ in) and then finish seaming.

WEFT SEQUENCE FOR A BLANKET
25 cm (9 ¾ in) gray pattern + black background
120 cm (47 ¼ in) white pattern + black background
25 cm (9 ¾ in) gray pattern + black background

REPEAT TO DESIRED LENGTH

× 2
× 2
× 2
× 2
× 2
× 2
× 2
× 2
× 2
× 2 = 6
BACKGROUND/ 6 PATTERNS

13 ENDS   13 ENDS   13 ENDS   13 ENDS   13 ENDS   13 ENDS   6 5 4 3 2 1

78 × 10 = 780 ENDS
PILLOW 78 X 4 = 312 ENDS

Black and white woolen woven with spot weave, p. 33.

Pillow woven in Jämtlandsdräll, p. 59.

Jämtlandsdräll (Crackle) Linen Rug

A section of the pattern on the blanket woven in Jämtlandsdräll (shown on page 58) makes a fine asymmetrical rug using rug linen for the weft.

TECHNIQUE
Jämtlandsdräll, 4 shafts and 6 treadles

MATERIALS

WARP	12/6 cotton rug warp black 522, approx. 2,950 m/kg Bocken's Yarns, Holma-Helsingland
WEFT	Hems: 8/5 linen warp yarn black 522 Background: 4/6 rug linen, black 522 Pattern: rug linen, moleskin 462 400 m/kg
REED	40/10 (10/in), 1 end per heddle, 1 end per dent = 4 ends/cm (10 epi)
WIDTH IN REED	approx. 62.5 cm (24 ½ in)
FINISHED WIDTH	approx. 60 cm (23 ¾ in)
WEFT SETT	6 background picks + pattern/2 cm (¾ in)
NUMBER OF ENDS	249
SELVEDGES	2 ends per dent at each side
WARP REQUIRED	Per meter: 90 g (3.2 oz)
WEFT REQUIRED	Per meter: 500 g (17.6 oz) of each color

WEAVING AND FINISHING
Weave about 6 cm (2 ½ in) in plain weave for the hem using 8/5 linen warp. Lay weft in with small arcs and pack in so that the warp is covered. Weave the pattern following the treadling sequence until piece is desired length. Be careful when throwing in the weft so that the selvedge stays firm. Lay in the rug linen diagonally and stretched out and then beat the shed Finish with the hem. Zigzag the edges. Sew down hems by hand.

WEFT
× = RUG LINEN, BLACK
■ = RUG LINEN, MOLESKIN

REPEAT TO
DESIRED LENGTH

× 4

HEM

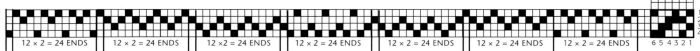

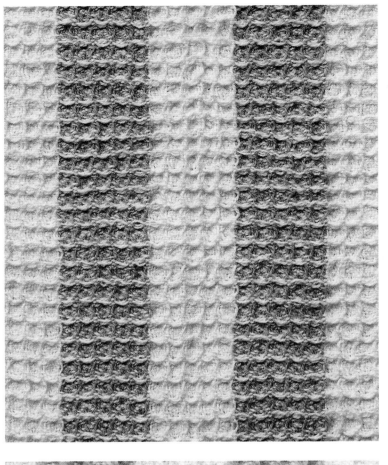

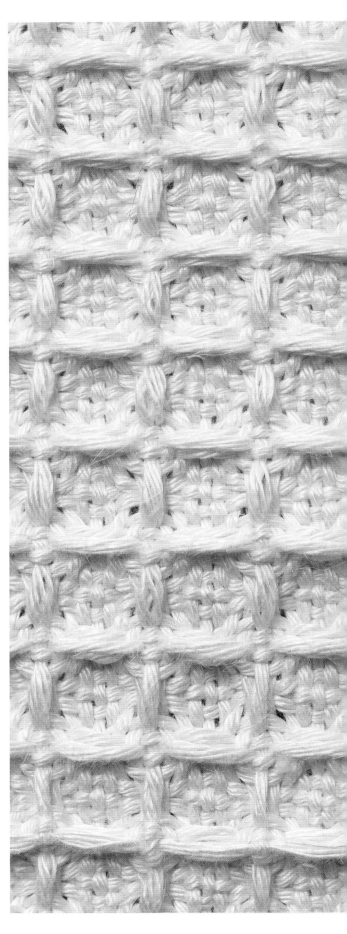

Waffle Weave

The name tells you just what this weave structure is, a weave with small hollows, like a waffle. When the weaving is washed, the pattern becomes even more distinctive. This "bubbly" weave is excellent for hand towels, but also for a heavy linen rug to massage your feet, a wool pillow, or a soft blanket for a child to curl up in.

Waffle Weave Hand Towels

Cottolin is a blend of cotton and linen that is perfect for hand towels because it is soft and moisture absorbing. These waffle weave towels need little care, just washing and using. They'll become more beautiful with each wash.

TECHNIQUE
Like-sided waffle weave, 5 shafts and 6 treadles
Upper tie-up: Contramarch or rubber band for each shaft.

MATERIALS

WARP	22/2 Cottolin ecru 0293, gray 9820 or ecru 0293, pink 273, 6,400 m/kg Borg's Weaving Yarns
WEFT	Same yarns as for warp
REED	40/10 (10/in), 1 end per heddle, 2 ends per dent = 8 ends/1 cm (20 epi)
SELVEDGES	3 ends per dent 2 times at each side
WIDTH IN REED	55 cm (21 ¾ in)
FINISHED WIDTH	49 cm (19 ¼ in), approx. 42 cm (16 ½ in) after washing at 60°C/140°F
WEFT SETT	approx. 10 picks/1 cm (25 epi)
NUMBER OF ENDS	440 (200 ends ecru + 240 ends gray (or pink)
WARP REQUIRED	Per meter: 32 g (1.1 oz) ecru, 38 g (1.3 oz) gray (or pink)
WEFT REQUIRED	Per meter: for striped towels approx. 86 g (3 oz); for checked towels approx. 43 g (1.5 oz) of each color

WEAVING
Use a temple and move it up frequently. Weave either squared checks or stripes with some of the warp colors. Weave 80 cm (31 ½ in) per hand towel, including 5 cm (2 in) for the hem. After washing, the hemmed towel will shrink to approx. 58 cm (22 ¾ in).

CARE AND FINISHING
Machine wash the entire length of towel fabric at 60°C/140°F to shrink the piece to the proper firmness. Cut the toweling with approx. 62 cm (24 ½ in) for each towel.

Note You can also weave the hand towels with an unlike-sided waffle weave structure using 4 shafts and 5 treadles. See the following instructions: Waffle weave with cotton on page 71 and Linen rug in waffle weave on page 72. In that case, you won't need the contramarch. Alternatively, you can hang each shaft with a rubber band.

WARP SEQUENCE

GRAY OR PINK	40		40	= 240 ENDS
ECRU		40		= 200 ENDS
	× 5			= 440 ENDS

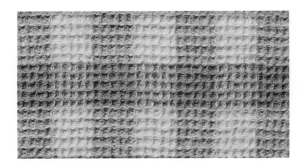

LIKE-SIDED WAFFLE WEAVE

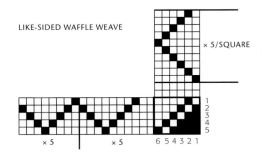

*Waffle weave hand
towels*

Cotton Waffle Weaves

A pretty hand towel or a soft blanket. Waffle weave woven with a thick cotton yarn can be used for so many projects.

TECHNIQUE
Unlike-sided waffle weave, 4 shafts and 5 treadles

MATERIALS

WARP	2/2 Cotton lime 5219, bleached 5020, turquoise 5218, 1,600 m/kg Borg's Weaving Yarns
WEFT	lime 5219, bleached 5020, same yarn as for warp
REED	40/10 (10/in), 1 end per heddle, 1 end per dent = 4 ends/1 cm (10 epi)
WIDTH IN REED	90 cm (35 ½ in)
FINISHED WIDTH	approx. 80 cm (31 ½ in)
WEFT SETT	approx. 4 picks/1 cm (10 ppi)
NUMBER OF ENDS	360 (200 lime, 96 bleached, 64 turquoise)
WARP REQUIRED	Per meter: 125 g (4.4 oz) lime, 60 g (2.1 oz) bleached, 40 g (1.4 oz) turquoise
WEFT REQUIRED	One towel approx. 120 cm (47 ¼ in): 70 g (2.5 oz) lime, approx. 210 g (7.35 oz) bleached

WEAVING
Use a temple. Avoid splicing the weft yarn when throwing the weft with long floats.

FINISHING
Finish by sewing blanket stitch along both sides or turn under a narrow hem.

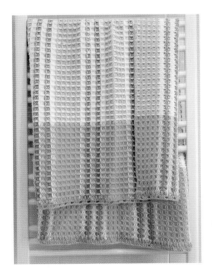

WARP SEQUENCE

LIME	40					40				40	= 200
BLEACHED		8		8		8		8		8	8	= 96
TURQUOISE			8		8			8		8		= 64

⌐ x 3 = 240 ENDS ⌐

8 ENDS   8 ENDS   5 4 3 2 1

1
2
3
4

Waffle Weave Linen Rug

For this rug, we tried to weave as thickly as possible, having chosen rug linen for the warp and weft. It made a firm rug with an exciting structure. Use it beside the bathtub or as a bedside rug.

TECHNIQUE
Unlike-sided waffle weave, 4 shafts and 5 treadles

MATERIALS

WARP	4/6 rug linen
	Half-bleached 400 m/kg
	Bocken's Yarns, Holma-Helsingland
WEFT	Hems: half-bleached 8/5 linen warp;
	rug linen as for warp
REED	30/10 (8/in), 1 end per heddle, 1 end
	per dent = 3 ends/1 cm (7.5 epi)
WIDTH IN REED	69.5 cm (27 ¼ in)
FINISHED WIDTH	67 cm (26 ½ in)
WEFT SETT	approx. 3 picks/1 cm (7.5 ppi) (weave
	the squares a bit longer than wide)
NUMBER OF ENDS	208
WARP REQUIRED	Per meter: approx. 525 g (18.5 oz)
WEFT REQUIRED	Per meter: approx. 525 g (18.5 oz)

WEAVING
Weave the hem with treadles 3, 4 with half-bleached 8/5 linen warp thread for about 8 cm (3 ¼ in). After completing hem, weave in waffle weave to desired length. Finish with hem.

FINISHING
The heavy warp ends lie in groups of 4. Pull every other group into the channel formed by the weft yarn. Tie the remaining ends 2 by 2. Fold under and sew the hems by hand (see detail picture).

CARE
Wash the rug by hand and dry flat.

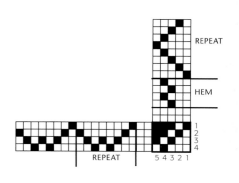

A beautiful length of waffle weave fabric to sew into a fine bathrobe, p. 76.

Waffle Weave Bathrobe

Weave a length of checked waffle weave (see instructions on page 67) and sew the fabric into a nice bathrobe. We wove 120 squares = approx. 6 m (6 ½ yd) or 4.8 m (5 ¼ yd finished fabric). To be on the safe side, we wove a few extra squares to make sure we could match the pattern when seaming. The blocks are squared to make it easier to match patterns in every direction.

Baste the bathrobe and then machine-stitch it with the wrong side facing or pin the pieces together and seam by hand using fine whip stitching with the right side facing so that the squares match as you like. Width of the fabric after finishing: approx. 40 cm (15 ¾ in). Size: Medium.

- Machine wash the fabric at 60˚C/140˚F.
- Keep in the mind that the fabric is non-reversible. Mark the right side of each piece with a strand of yarn.
- Divide the fabric into 6 pieces following the schematics below. Save some of the fabric or a few extra squares of each length until you are sure that the patterns match. Extra fabric can be cut away after seaming.
- Seam the back pieces at center back.

- Sew the shoulder seams.
- Fold a V-neck line on the front pieces and stitch all around on the wrong side. The turned-under fabric will be used as the facing.
- Sew in the sleeves to front and back.
- Sew the side and sleeve seams.
- Fold under the front edges, the lower edge, and the sleeve edges and hem with simple hem stitching.

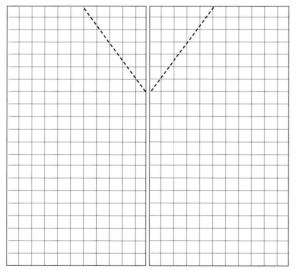

FRONT, EACH PIECE HAS 11 X 21 SQUARES

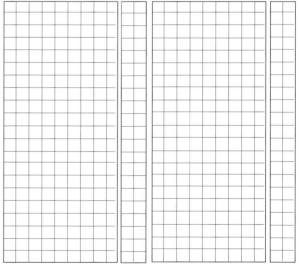

2 X BACK PIECES
TRIM PIECE 2 SQUARES WIDE FROM EACH BACK
PIECE TO USE FOR THE BELT.

BELT
SEAM THE TWO PIECES INTO ONE LENGTH.
FOLD DOUBLE AND FOLD UNDER HEM AND
THEN HAND SEW WITH FINE STITCHES ON
RIGHT SIDE.

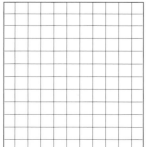

2 X SLEEVES
EACH PIECE HAS 11 X 12 SQUARES

Woolen Waffle Weave

A checked waffle weave, like the cottolin hand towels on page 67, but now woven with wool into a fine pillow. Weave a wider fabric for a blanket.

TECHNIQUE
Unlike-sided waffle weave, 4 shafts and 5 treadles

MATERIALS

WARP	Tuna 6/2 wool yarn green 3333, white 3001, 3,100 m/kg Borg's Weaving Yarns
WEFT	Same yarn as for warp
REED	30/10 (8/in), 1 end per heddle, 2 ends per dent = 6 ends/1 cm (15 epi)
SELVEDGES	3 ends per dent 2 times at each side
WIDTH IN REED	58 cm (22 ¾ in)
FINISHED WIDTH	approx. 47 cm (18 ½ in) after washing at 40°C/104°F
WEFT SETT	approx. 6 picks/1 cm (15 ppi)
NUMBER OF ENDS	352 (192 green, 160 white)
WARP REQUIRED	Per meter: approx. 65 g (2.3 oz) green, 55 g (1.9 oz) white
WEFT REQUIRED	Per pillow: approx. 70 g (2.5 oz) green, approx. 60 g (2.1 oz) white

WEAVING
Weave squared as for the warp. For each pillow, weave approx. 110 cm (43 ¼ in). Machine-wash at 40°C/104°F. Fold fabric for each pillow in half. Sew side seams by hand. Insert a pillow form and then finish seaming.

WARP SEQUENCE

GREEN	32		32	= 192
WHITE		32		= 160
		× 5		= 352 ENDS

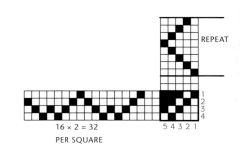

REPEAT

16 × 2 = 32

PER SQUARE

5 4 3 2 1

1
2
3
4

Twills

Twills build the patterning diagonally. They can be wavy, dia-
mond, goose-eye, or herringbone patterns depending on how
they are threaded and treadled. Two different twill structures
are used for effect in curtains; for a blanket the goose-eye is
centered on each block, and, for a general use fabric, the
herringbone pattern plays between stripes and squares.

Goose-eye Blanket

Weave a twill in blocks with the goose-eye pattern reversing in each square.

TECHNIQUE
Goose-eye, 4 shafts and 4 treadles

MATERIALS

WARP	Tuna 6/2 wool yarn, 3,100 m/kg white 3001, gray 3023, beige 3763, brown 3762, green 3040 Borg's Weaving Yarns
WEFT	Same yarn as for warp
REED	30/10 (8/in), 1 end per heddle, 2 ends per dent = 6 ends/1 cm (15 epi)
SELVEDGES	2 ends per dent 2 times at each side
WIDTH IN REED	approx. 146 cm (57 ½ in)
WEFT SETT	1 block = 8 cm (3 ¼ in)
NUMBER OF ENDS	874
WARP REQUIRED	Per meter: 140 g (4.9 oz) white, 50 g (1.8 oz) gray, 50 g (1.8 oz) beige, 30 g (1 oz) green, 30 g (1 oz) brown
WEFT REQUIRED	Per blanket: 215 g (7.5 oz) white, 60 g (2.1 oz) each gray, beige, green, brown

WEAVING
Weave about 10 cm (4 in) for a header. Advance fabric onto beam, leaving about 30 cm (11 ¾ in) unwoven. Weave a few shots on the first blanket. Twist the fringes to the right with 8 ends, 4 ends in each hand. When weaving several blankets, leave 30 cm (11 ¾ in) between each blanket. Twist the fringes when still on the loom.

FINISHING
Machine-wash on wool setting 40°C/104°F with mild wool wash or take blankets in to be professionally finished.

PATTERN BLOCKS, THREADING

DYED YARNS	46		46
WHITE		46	
		× 18	

WARP SEQUENCE

GRAY	46						46		= 138 ENDS
WHITE		46		46		46		46		46	= 414 ENDS
BEIGE			46						46	= 138 ENDS
GREEN				46						= 92 ENDS
BROWN						46				= 92 ENDS

× 2

WEFT SEQUENCE IN CM (1 CM=⅜ IN) X 3, TOTAL LENGTH OF WEAVING 184 CM (2 YD)

GRAY	8				
WHITE		8		8		8		8*
BEIGE			8		
GREEN				8	
BROWN					8

The white square is not woven on the last repeat.

WARP AND WEFT
■ = DYED YARNS
O = WHITE

× 4
× 5
× 4
× 5

4 × 4   7 ENDS   4 × 5   4 × 4   7 ENDS   4 × 5   4 3 2 1
WHITE   DYED YARNS

1
2
3
4

Colorful Herringbone Weaves

By breaking the threading when the diagonal line turns, you get a pattern called herringbone. Here is a check weave in cheerful colors. Weave this fabric for pillows, towels or a lovely table runner.

TECHNIQUE
Broken twill, herringbone, 4 shafts and 4 treadles

MATERIALS

WARP	22/2 Nialin
	green 2069, purple 2026, lime 2041,
	orange 2013, turquoise 2032,
	pale yellow 2008, 6,600 m/kg
	Bocken's Yarns, Holma-Helsingland
WEFT	Same as for warp yarns
REED	55/10 (13.5/in), 1 end per heddle,
	2 ends per dent = 11 ends/1 cm
	(27.5 epi)
WIDTH IN REED	53.5 cm (21 in)
FINISHED WIDTH	50 cm (19 ¾ in)
WEFT SETT	10 picks/1 cm (25 ppi)
NUMBER OF ENDS	590
WARP REQUIRED	Per meter: approx. 35 g (1.2 oz) green,
	5 g (.2 oz) purple, 25 g (.88 oz) lime,
	5 g (.2 oz) orange, 25 g (.88 oz)
	turquoise, 5 g (.2 oz) pale yellow

WEFT REQUIRED   Per meter: approx. 25 g (.88 oz) green, 5 g (.2 oz) purple, 25 g (.88 oz) lime, 5 g (.2 oz) orange, 25 g (.88 oz) turquoise, 5 g (.2 oz) pale yellow

WEAVING
Weave following the weft sequence. Make sure the weft sett is correct.

PILLOWS: Weave approx. 106 cm (41 ¾ in) for each pillow. Fold under and then machine-stitch hems. Fold the pillow fabric, overlapping the hems so that the flap is on top. Sew on 5-6 snaps. Turn the pillow cover inside out. Machine-stitch each side seam. The pillow cover should be 50 cm (19 ¾ in) wide. Button up cover and turn right side out. Insert a pillow form.

WARP SEQUENCE

GREEN	50					50	= 200 ENDS
PURPLE		10					= 30 ENDS
LIME			50				= 150 ENDS
ORANGE				10			= 30 ENDS
TURQUOISE					50		= 150 ENDS
PALE YELLOW						10	= 30 ENDS

× 3   = 590 ENDS

WEFT SEQUENCE

5 cm (2 in)	green	
1 cm (⅜ in)	purple	
5 cm (2 in)	lime	repeat
1 cm (⅜ in)	orange	
5 cm (2 in)	turquoise	
1 cm (⅜ in)	pale yellow	

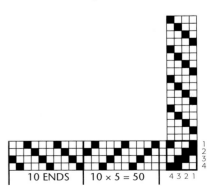

10 ENDS   10 × 5 = 50   4 3 2 1

All of the pillows in the book.

Sheer Curtains in Two Twill Patterns

A twill-woven curtain panel with one block threaded in a "V" and the other threaded from shafts 1 to 4. The zig-zag point twill pattern waves subtly in the light stripes while the goose-eye design shows more distinctly in the dark stripes. You can weave these curtains with a single or 2-ply linen yarn for the warp.

TECHNIQUE
Goose-eye and point twill, 4 shafts and 4 treadles

MATERIALS

WARP	16/1 Linen unbleached 10,060 m/kg and half-bleached 11,240 m/kg OR 35/2 linen unbleached 9,200 and half-bleached 10,000 m/kg Bocken's Yarns, Holma-Helsingland
WEFT	Half-bleached 16/1 linen as for warp
REED	110/10 (27/in), 1 end per heddle, 1 end per dent = 11 ends/1 cm (27.5 epi)
WIDTH IN REED	70 cm (27 ½ in)
FINISHED WIDTH	68 cm (26 ¾ in)
WEFT SETT	11 picks/1 cm (27.5 ppi)
NUMBER OF ENDS	776 (440 unbleached, 336 half-bleached)
WARP REQUIRED	Per meter: 16 linen: approx. 45 g (1.6 oz) unbleached, 30 g (1 oz) half-bleached 35/2 linen: approx. 50 g (1.8 oz) unbleached, approx. 35 g (1.2 oz) half-bleached
WEFT REQUIRED	Per meter: approx. 70 g (2.5 oz) half-bleached 16/1 linen

WEAVING
Use a temple and move it up frequently. Make sure weft sett is correct throughout. See also: "Weaving with Linen" p. 114.

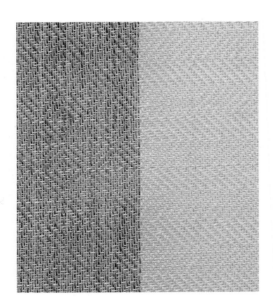

WARP SEQUENCE

UNBLEACHED	110		110
HALF-BLEACHED		112	

× 3

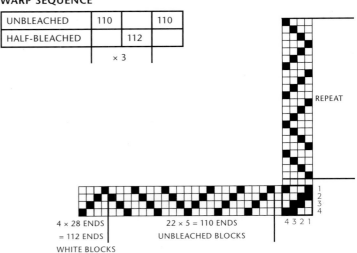

REPEAT

4 × 28 ENDS = 112 ENDS WHITE BLOCKS

22 × 5 = 110 ENDS UNBLEACHED BLOCKS

Color Effects

If you combine different weave structures with various colors in the warp and weft, you can get the most fantastic results. One of the most common color effect weaves is hound's-tooth which, when woven in a fine check pattern, makes fabrics suitable for everything from pillows to runners, placemats or colorful towels.

The twill linen rugs have another warp sequence for a pattern variation. The pillows in the softest velour yarns are woven in plain weave in yet another color effect pattern—log cabin.

Checked Hound's-Tooth for Many Projects

The hound's-tooth pattern is a color effect like-sided twill weave with four dark and four light ends in the warp and weft. We've combined it with blue and turquoise blocks for our design. Weave pillows, towels, or a runner for the table—all in the same weave structure.

TECHNIQUE
Like-sided twill, color effect, 4 shafts and 4 treadles

MATERIALS

WARP	22/2 Nialin blue 2028, navy blue 2031, white 2000, 6,600 m/kg Bocken's Yarns, Holma-Helsingland
WEFT	22/2 Nialin blue 2028, ultramarine 2029, white 2000, turquoise 2032, 6,600 m/kg Bocken's Yarns, Holma-Helsingland
REED	55/10 (approx. 14/in), 1 end per heddle, 2 ends per dent = 11 ends/ 1 cm (27.5 epi)

WIDTH IN REED	55 cm (21 ¾ in)
FINISHED WIDTH	53 cm (21 in)
WEFT SETT	10 picks/1 cm (25 ppi)
NUMBER OF ENDS	612
WARP REQUIRED	Per meter: 50 g (1.8 oz) blue, 25 g (.88 oz) navy, 20 g (.7 oz) white
WEFT REQUIRED	Per meter: 25 g (.88 oz) blue, 20 g (.7 oz) white, 25 g (.88 oz) ultramarine, 25 g (.88 oz) turquoise

WEAVING
Use a temple and move it up frequently. Make sure weft sett is correct throughout.

WARP SEQUENCE

BLUE	36							36	= 324
NAVY		4		4		4		4		4		= 160
WHITE			4		4		4		4			= 128

72 × 8 = 576 ENDS

WEFT SEQUENCE, ONE REPEAT

3 cm (1 ¼ in)	blue 2028	
4 picks	white 2000	
4 picks	ultramarine 2029	} × 3
4 picks	white 2000	
3 cm (1 ¼ in)	turquoise 2032	
4 picks	white 2000	
4 picks	ultramarine 2029	} × 3
4 picks	white 2000	

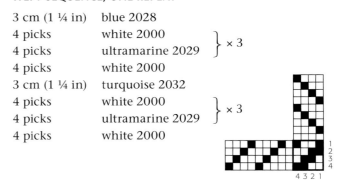

Plain Weave Color Effect Pillows

Color effect log cabin is woven in plain weave. It is threaded and woven with alternating light and dark threads that interchange for a plaited effect. By varying the weft sequence you can produce a whole collection of pillows: checked, vertical stripes with color effect patterns or stripes with one color of weft. The bottom pillow in the photo to left is woven in hound's-tooth (see page 92).

TECHNIQUE
Plain weave, color effect, 4 shafts and 2 treadles

MATERIALS

WARP	Velour yarn white 1020, medium blue 1295, dark blue 1324, 1,800 m/kg Borg's Weaving Yarns
WEFT	Same yarns as for warp
REED	45/10 (12/in), 1 end per heddle, 1 end per dent = 4.5 ends/1 cm (11.25 epi)
WIDTH IN REED	43 cm (17 in)
FINISHED WIDTH	40 cm (15 ¾ in)
WEFT SETT	approx. 9 picks/2 cm (11.25 ppi)
NUMBER OF ENDS	194
WARP REQUIRED	Per meter: 40 g (1.4 oz) white, approx. 55 g (1.9 oz) medium blue, 20 g (.7 oz) dark blue

WARP SEQUENCE

WHITE	1				1	= 72
MEDIUM BLUE	1	2		2	1	= 92
DARK BLUE			6			= 30
	× 12 = 24		× 5	× 12 = 24		

WEFT REQUIRED	Per meter: 110 g (3.85 oz) with one color Weft sequence 2: 55 g (1.9 oz) white, 55 g (1.9 oz) medium blue Weft sequence 3: as for warp

WEAVING
Use a temple and move it up frequently. Make sure weft sett is correct.

WEFT SEQUENCE 1
Use only dark blue.

WEFT SEQUENCE 2
12 picks treadle 1 medium blue, treadle 2 white
12 picks with colors changing places
treadle 1 white, treadle 2 medium blue

WEFT SEQUENCE 3, CHECKED PILLOW (AS FOR THREADING)
2 squares with color effect:
12 picks treadle 1 white, treadle 2 medium blue
12 picks with colors changing places
treadle 1 medium blue, treadle 2 white
2 picks medium blue
6 picks dark blue
2 picks medium blue

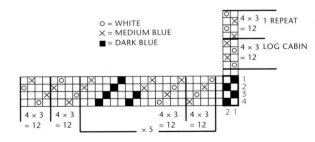

O = WHITE
X = MEDIUM BLUE
■ = DARK BLUE

Linen curtains woven in damask, p. 114.

Color effect pillows in plain weave, p. 95.

Color effect linen rugs, p. 98.

Color Effect Linen Rugs

A new color effect. In this case, the warp has 4 dark ends and 2 white ends. One rug is woven with only a dark weft while the other is woven with 4 dark and 2 light as in the warp. Rugs woven completely in linen will be smooth and sturdy, like jewelry for the floor.

TECHNIQUE
Like-sided twill, color effect, 4 shafts and 4 treadles

MATERIALS

WARP	4/6 rug linen
	blue 1004, half-bleached, 400 m/kg
	Bocken's Yarns, Holma-Helsingland
WEFT	Same yarns as for warp (split the rug linen for the hems)
REED	30/10 (8/in), 1 end per heddle, 1 end per dent = 3 ends/1 cm (7.5 epi)
WIDTH IN REED	approx. 57.5 cm (22 ½ in)
FINISHED WIDTH	approx. 56 cm (22 in)
WEFT SETT	3 picks/1 cm (7.5 ppi)
NUMBER OF ENDS	172 (116 blue, 56 white)
WARP REQUIRED	Per meter: 290 g (10.2 oz) blue, 140 g (4.9 oz) white

WEFT REQUIRED	Per meter:
	single color weft: approx. 435 g (15.3 oz);
	2 weft colors: 290 g (10.2 oz) blue, 140 g (4.9 oz) white

WEAVING
Split the rug linen to 3 plies for weaving the hems and weave hem for approx. 6 cm (2 ½ in). Weave following the weft sequence to desired length. End with a hem.

Zigzag the edge several times. Fold hem under and sew down by hand.

WARP SEQUENCE

BLUE	4		4	= 116
WHITE		2		= 56
	× 28			

Weft in same sequence as warp.

Only dark weft.

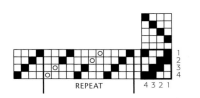

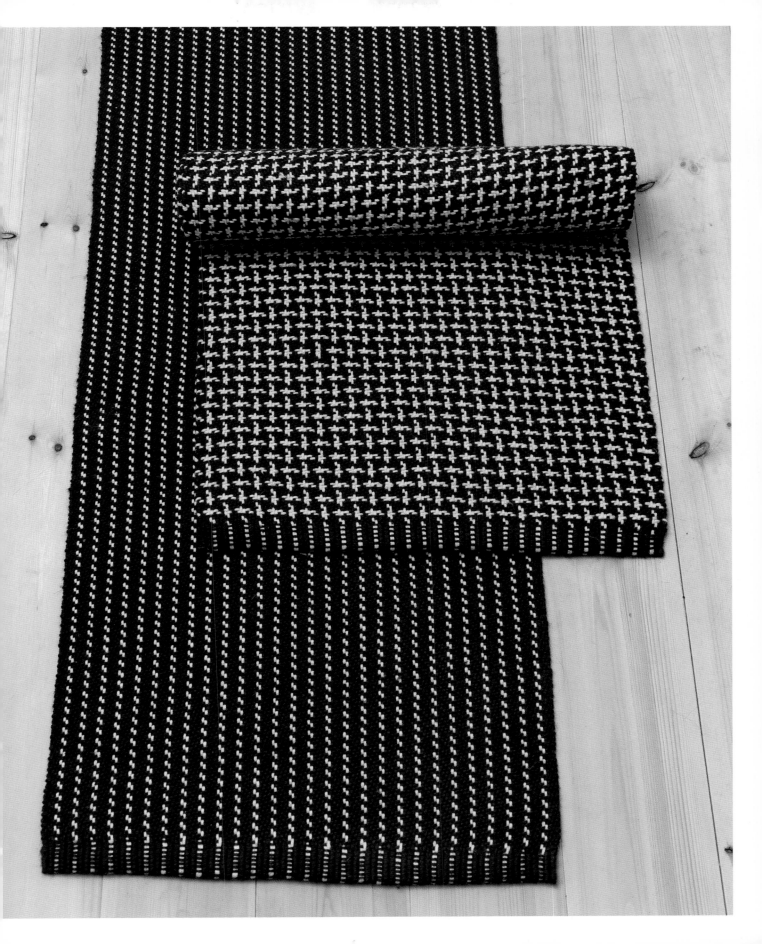

M's and O's
and Halvdräll

Both M's and O's and halvdräll are formed in blocks and often have patterns derived from "true" block damask. Halvdräll shows two completely different characteristics in a general-use fabric and a rug with small rosette patterns The M's and O's towels are designed on a striped warp where the weft can make both checked and striped weaves.

Halvdräll "Star" Fabric

In halvdräll weaves the floats are tied down. The technique is often used to weave towels and hand towels with patterns similar to "true" block damask. You only need four shafts and treadles. The technique shown here ties down a floating white weft to make small stars. Weave this fabric for a table runner, fine pillows, or upholstery.

TECHNIQUE
Halvdräll, 4 shafts and 4 treadles

MATERIALS

WARP	16/2 cotton
	black 522, 12,960 m/kg
	Bocken's Yarns, Holma-Helsingland
WEFT	Same yarn as for warp, black with single strand weft, bleached with 3 strands held together for weft
REED	70/10 (18/in),
	black: 1 end per heddle, 2 ends per dent = 14 ends/1 cm (35 epi)
	white: 3 ends per heddle, 3 ends per dent = 21 ends/1 cm (52.5 epi)
WIDTH IN REED	approx. 47 cm (18 ½ in)
FINISHED WIDTH	approx. 45 cm (17 ¾ in)
WEFT SETT	11 picks/1 cm (27.5 ppi) (8 plain weave + 1 star)
NUMBER OF ENDS	734 (536 black, 198 white)
WARP REQUIRED	Per meter: approx. 45 g (1.6 oz) black, approx. 16 g (.56 oz) white
WEFT REQUIRED	Per meter: approx. 40 g (1.4 oz) black, 25 g (.88 oz) white

WEAVING
Use a temple and move it up frequently. Make sure weft sett is correct.

WARP SEQUENCE

BLACK	8		8	= 536
WHITE		3		= 198
	× 66			

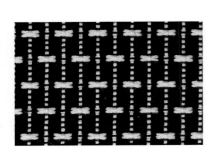

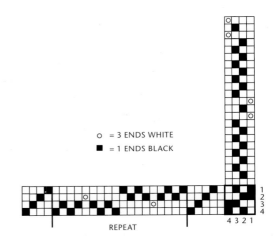

o = 3 ENDS WHITE
■ = 1 ENDS BLACK

1
2
3
4

4 3 2 1

REPEAT

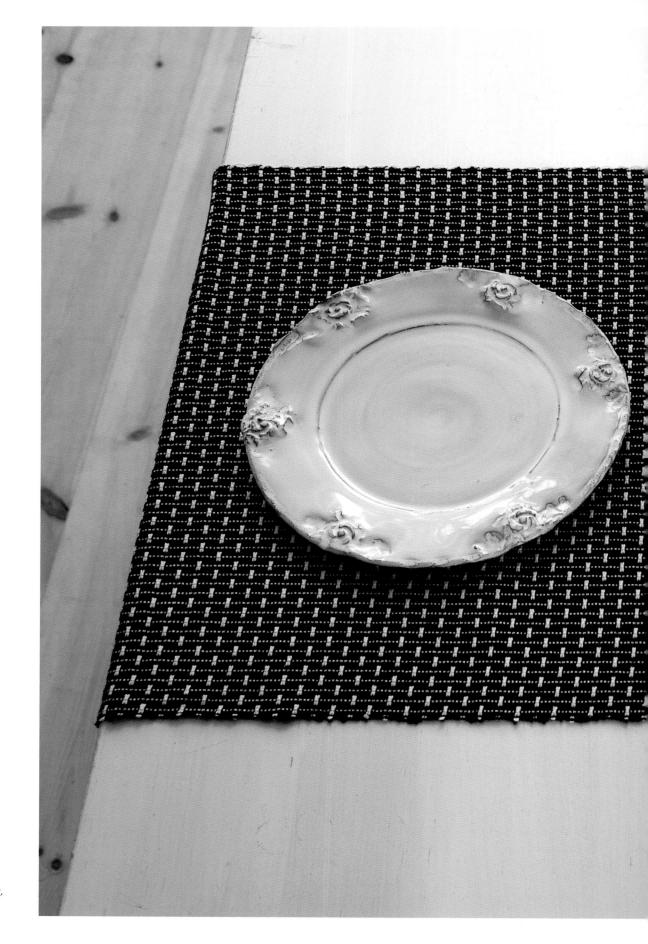

Halvdräll star fabric,
p. 103.

Halvdräll Wool Rug

The small stars in halvdräll on page 103 are transformed here into fine woolen rosettes on a wool rug.

TECHNIQUE
Halvdräll, 4 shafts and 4 treadles

MATERIALS

WARP	Boiled 8/3 linen warp, 1,400 m/kg
	Bocken's Yarns, Holma-Helsingland
WEFT	1.9/6 wool rug yarn
	natural, moleskin 462,
	black 522, 300 m/kg
	Bocken's Yarns, Holma-Helsingland
REED	20/10 (5/in), 1 end per heddle, 1 end
	per dent = 2 ends/1 cm (5 epi)
WIDTH IN REED	80 cm (31 ½ in)
FINISHED WIDTH	approx. 74 cm (29 ¼ in)
WEFT SETT	Plain weave: 3 picks/1 cm (3/8 in)
	Pattern: 6 patterns + 6 plain weave
	picks approx. 2.3 cm (7/8 in)
NUMBER OF ENDS	160
WARP REQUIRED	Per meter: approx. 120 g (4.2 oz)
WEFT REQUIRED	Per rug: 1.5 kg (3.7 lb) natural,
	1.2 kg (2.6 lb) moleskin, 200 g (7 oz)
	black

WEAVING
Begin by weaving approx. 20 cm (8 in) with rags that will be removed after the weaving is complete). Weave 8 picks with linen warp thread, arching weft well.

Weave following the weft sequence. Make sure weft sett is correct.

FINISHING
Keep the 8 linen weft threads. Braids: Tie in 4 linen warp ends doubled length together with 4 ends from the rug. Turn and braid. The rug in the photo has a four end-braid: Braid as usual with three of the ends, lay the outermost end under at each side on alternate twists. End with 2 half hitches tying one strand around the others.

WEFT SEQUENCE FOR ONE RUG
Make sure there is 20 cm (8 in) for the fringe
8 picks with linen warp

6 picks gray wool rug yarn
22 cm (8 ¾ in) with gray background and black pattern
End the border with 4 picks gray

4 picks white
178 cm (70 in) with white background and gray pattern
End with 4 picks white

4 picks gray
22 cm (8 ¾ in) with gray background and black pattern
End border with 6 picks gray
8 picks linen warp
20 cm (8 in) fringe

○ = PATTERN TREADLES
■ = PLAIN WEAVE

PLAIN WEAVE

BORDER II

PLAIN WEAVE

BORDER I

PLAIN WEAVE

1
2
3
4

18 × 8 = 144 ENDS   4 3 2 1

M's and O's Guest Towel

M's and O's are formed in two blocks that make little wave shapes in the block pattern. One block is a tightly woven plain weave and the other has floats over 4 warp ends. We have woven our towels with two different weft yarns: one thin and one heavy tow yarn.

TECHNIQUE
M's and O's, 4 shafts and 4 treadles

MATERIALS

WARP	22/2 Cottolin bleached and unbleached approx. 6,400 m/kg Borg's Weaving Yarns
WEFT	8/1 Tow yarn unbleached 4,850 m/kg and half-bleached approx. 5,400 m/kg Borg's Weaving Yarns OR 1.5/1 Linen tow unbleached and half-bleached approx. 900 m/kg Bocken's Yarns, Holma-Helsingland
REED	50/10 (12/in), 1 end per heddle, 2 ends per dent = 10 ends/1 cm (25 epi)
WIDTH IN REED	approx. 43 cm (17 in)
FINISHED WIDTH	approx. 38 cm (15 in)
WEFT SETT	Tow: approx. 8 picks/1 cm (20 ppi) 1.5 Linen: 4-5 picks/1 cm (10-12.5 ppi)
NUMBER OF ENDS	432 (224 unbleached, 208 bleached)

WARP REQUIRED	Per meter: approx. 40 g (1.4 oz) unbleached, approx. 35 g (1.2 oz) bleached
WEFT REQUIRED	Per meter: 8/1 tow, single color: approx. 75 g (2.6 oz) unbleached or 65 g (2.3 oz) half-bleached checked pattern: approx. 35 g (1.2 oz) bleached and half-bleached 1.5/1 Linen tow single color: approx. 240 g (8.4 oz) checked pattern: approx. 120 g (4.2 oz) of each color

WEAVING
Use a temple and move it up frequently. Make sure weft sett is correct. Weave the towels with a single color or checked by shifting between the two blocks.

WARP SEQUENCE

UNBLEACHED	16		16	= 224
BLEACHED		16		= 208
	× 13			432 ENDS

8/1 TOW = 12 PICKS/SQUARE
1.5 LINEN = 6 PICKS/SQUARE

o = BLEACHED
■ = UNBLEACHED

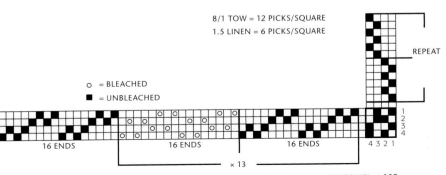

REPEAT

16 ENDS   16 ENDS   16 ENDS

× 13

Guest towels woven in M's and O's, p. 109. Crocheted potholder.

Block Damask
(True Dräll)

In a true block damask, the weft-effect and warp-effect structures create the block pattern. Each block requires the number of treadles as there are warp ends in the interlacement. In our four damask projects, two different four-shaft twill structures have been used: some a diagonal twill, others a broken twill also called "false satin." We played with the weft and warp effects and made horizontal stripes, vertical stripes, and checked damasks.

Linen Curtains in Damask

Two textures with the same weave – a vertically striped damask. The threading is in two blocks but the treadling uses only one. The weft-effect and warp-effect produce a diagonal twill with a fine interplay of the lines between the stripes.

TECHNIQUE
Damask, 8 shafts and 4 treadles

MATERIALS

WARP	Singles linen:
	half-bleached 16/1 linen, 11,240 m/kg
	OR
	2-ply linen:
	half-bleached 16/2 linen, 5,520 m/kg
	Bocken's Yarns, Holma-Helsingland
WEFT	Same weft as for the warp
REED	Singles linen:
	60/10 (15/in), 1 end per heddle, 2 ends
	per dent = 12 ends/1 cm (30 epi)
	2-ply linen:
	50/10 (12/in), 1 end per heddle, 2 ends
	per dent = 10 ends/1 cm (25 epi)
WIDTH IN REED	approx. 63 cm (24 ¾ in)
FINISHED WIDTH	approx. 62 cm (24 ½ in)
WEFT SETT	singles linen: 12 picks/1 cm (30 ppi)
	2-ply linen: 8 picks/1 cm (20 ppi)
NUMBER OF ENDS	Singles linen: 760
	2-ply linen: 632
WARP REQUIRED	Per meter: singles linen: approx. 68 g
	(2.4 oz); 2-ply linen: 115 g (4 oz)
WEFT REQUIRED	Per meter: singles linen: approx. 68 g
	(2.4 oz); 2-ply linen: approx. 95 g
	(3.35 oz)

WEAVING WITH LINEN

Linen is not an elastic yarn. You need to be careful to avoid unnecessary abrasion and stress when you warp, wind on, prepare the weave, and weave the fabric.

If the weaving is wider than 60 cm (23 ¾ in), we recommend that you make two or more warp chains. Be careful when beaming and space the beam sticks closely. Before you begin to weave, check to be sure the shafts and beater are at the right height, the warp threads are centered in the heddle eyes and the warp is centered in the reed. If the linen has become abraded while threading through the heddles and reed remove some before tying the front knots.

Lay in the weft at a diagonal when you weave. Try to avoid fussing with the selvedge ends. Beat in a closed shed = when the warp threads are parallel and the treadles are up. Use a temple and move it up frequently.

If the warp threads begin to snap, seem dry and brittle, you can carefully lay a damp towel over the warp at the back beam or brush with a dressing made from boiled flax seeds.

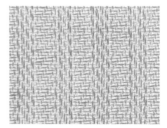

16/1 Linen yarn   *16/2 Linen yarn*

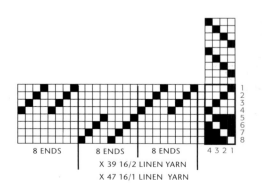

8 ENDS   8 ENDS   8 ENDS   4 3 2 1

X 39 16/2 LINEN YARN
X 47 16/1 LINEN YARN

Wool Blanket in Damask

Here we've turned the stripes and woven a horizontal damask with wool yarn. Four shafts are threaded straight through and the treadlings change between the two blocks. Exactly as for the curtains on page 114, there is a diagonal twill in weft-effect and warp-effect. The warp yarn is unwashed and the weft is washed. After the blanket has been soaked in warm water, the yarns draw together into soft waves on the surface.

TECHNIQUE
Damask, 4 shafts and 8 treadles

MATERIALS

WARP	Tuna 6/2 wool yarn white unwashed, approx. 3,100 m/kg Borg's Weaving Yarns
WEFT	Tuna 6/2 wool yarn white 3000, approx. 3,100 m/kg Borg's Weaving Yarns
REED	30/10 (8/in), 1 end per heddle, 2 ends per dent = 6 ends/1 cm (15 epi)
WIDTH IN REED	110 cm (43 ¼ in)
FINISHED WIDTH	104 cm (41 in)
WEFT SETT	6 picks/1 cm (15 ppi)
NUMBER OF ENDS	660
WARP REQUIRED	Per meter: approx. 215 g (7.5 oz)
WEFT REQUIRED	Per meter: approx. 215 g (7.5 oz)

WEAVING
Weave the hem in weft effect for approx. 6 cm (2 ½ in). Weave 8 picks of weft and warp effect to desired length. End with weft effect and hem.

FINISHING
Zigzag the edges and soak the blanket in lukewarm water overnight. Roll up into a towel and squeeze out excess water. Leave flat to dry. Hem by hand.

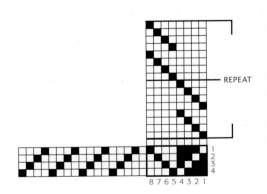

REPEAT

8 7 6 5 4 3 2 1

1 2 3 4

Checkerboard Wool Rug in Damask

Now both the threading and treadling are warp- and weft-effect and we can create a checkerboard damask. We've combined a tightly spaced linen warp with a strong warm red wool yarn for the weft.

TECHNIQUE
Block damask, 8 shafts and 8 treadles

MATERIALS

WARP	8/5 linen warp yarn
	black 522, 900 m/kg
	Bocken's Yarns, Holma-Helsingland
WEFT	1.9/6 wool rug yarn, approx. 300 m/kg
	red 2080
	hems: 8/5 linen warp yarn black
	Bocken's Yarns, Holma-Helsingland
REED	30/10 (8/in), 1 end per heddle, 2 ends
	per dent = 6 ends/cm (15 epi)
SELVEDGES	2 ends at each side unthreaded for
	a better edge. When weaving the weft
	goes over the selvedge on the way in
	the shed and under on the way out.
WIDTH IN REED	approx. 65.5 cm (25 ¾ in)
FINISHED WIDTH	approx. 64 cm (25 ¼ in)
WEFT SETT	4-5 picks/2 cm (5-6.25 ppi)
NUMBER OF ENDS	396
WARP REQUIRED	Per meter: approx. 450 g (15.5 oz)
WEFT REQUIRED	Per meter: approx. 500 g (17.6 oz)

WEAVING AND FINISHING

Weave approx. 8 cm (3 ¼ in) on treadles 1-4 for the hem. Weave in block pattern to desired length. Weave each block about 12 cm (4 ¾ in) long. The rug will draw in after cutting off the loom and pressing.

Knot the warp ends in pairs. Fold under and hem by hand.

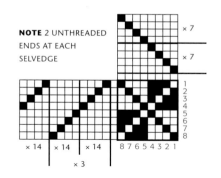

NOTE 2 UNTHREADED ENDS AT EACH SELVEDGE

× 7
× 7

1
2
3
4
5
6
7
8

× 14   × 14   × 14   8 7 6 5 4 3 2 1

× 3

Damask Table Runner

Here is a broken twill in two blocks. The interlacement points are more spread out in a broken twill than they are in a diagonal twill as in the previous damasks and the pattern is sometimes called false satin. Weave following the treadling sequence to make a lovely holiday runner or vary the design and weave the same number of each block for upholstery fabric.

TECHNIQUE
Block damask, 8 shafts and 8 treadles

MATERIALS

WARP	22/2 Nialin
	red 2080, 6,600 m/kg
	Bocken's Yarns, Holma-Helsingland
WEFT	8/1 Linen tow yarn
	black 522, 5,600 m/kg
	Bocken's Yarns, Holma-Helsingland
REED	70/10 (18/in), 1 end per heddle, 2 ends
	per dent = 14 ends/1 cm (35 epi)
WIDTH IN REED	approx. 48 cm (19 in)
FINISHED WIDTH	approx. 47 cm (18 ½ in)
WEFT SETT	10 picks/1 cm (25 ppi)
NUMBER OF ENDS	668

WARP REQUIRED	Per meter: approx. 105 g (3.8 oz)
WEFT REQUIRED	Per meter: approx. 100 g (3.5 oz)

WEAVING
Weave following the weft sequence. Begin by weaving a hem in the same block as the pattern begins with for approx. 4 cm (1 ½ in). Weave to desired length and end with 4 cm (1 ½ in) in the same block. Hem by hand.

PATTERN BALANCING

Right selvedge	4 ends
Group I 60 ends + group II = 120 ends x 5	600 ends
Group I 60 ends	60 ends
Left selvedge	4 ends
	= 668 ends

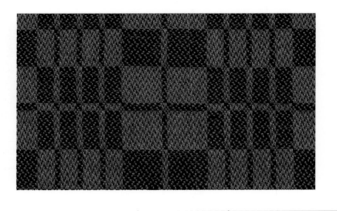

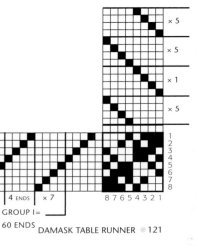

× 7	4 ENDS	× 7	12 ENDS	× 3	× 7	4 ENDS	× 7
GROUP I= 60 ENDS			GROUP II= 60 ENDS		GROUP I= 60 ENDS		

Finishings:
Twist a fringe, sew
buttonhole stitch all
around, sew a hem, or
line your weaving with a
sheepskin.

Index

Here are examples of how we've used the woven fabrics in this book. Many of them can be used several ways – you decide.

Projects Arranged According to Number of Shafts And Treadles

Sources for Materials

UNITED STATES

Vävstuga Weaving School
(413) 625-8241
www.vavstuga.com
office@vavstuga.com

Lone Star Loom Room
(888) 562-7012
www.lonestarloomroom.com
tkweaver1@gmail.com

Glimakra Looms-USA
(406) 442 0354 / 1-866-890-7314
www.glimakraUSA.com
info@glimakraUSA.com

The Mannings Handweaving School & Supply Center
(800) 233-7166 orders only
www.the-mannings.com
office@the-mannings.com

CANADA

Camilla Valley Farm Weavers' Supply
519-941-0736 phone
519-941-0804 fax
www.CamillaValleyFarm.com
nmanners@camillavalleyfarm.com

Objects shown in the photo settings:
Ceramic bowls page 19, Ingegerd Råman
Turned bowl page 40, Åke Landström
Pitcher and cups page 57, Anna Lindell
Iron work candle holder page 66, Lennart Larsson
Ceramic candle holders page 85, Sam Stigsson
Root basket page 93, Lola Zackrisson
Plates page 104, Kina Björklund
Candelabra page 121, designed by Bengt Lindberg